Beautiful America's

Seattle

Front Cover, Seattle

Published by
Beautiful America Publishing Company®
9725 S.W. Commerce Circle
Wilsonville, Oregon 97070

Library of Congress Cataloging in Publication Data
Beautiful America's Seattle

Library of Congress Catalog Number 89-17800

ISBN 0-89802-522-2
ISBN 0-89802-521-4 (Paperback)

International Fountain and the Space Needle

Beautiful America's
Seattle

Text by Ann Rule

Photography by Craig Tuttle

Table of Contents

Introduction

I have lived in so many cities in so many states, but from my first glimpse of Seattle on a misty November Sunday too many years ago to note, I knew I was *home* at last. Seattle was the "Queen City" then; now she has spread her iridescent wings and become the "Emerald City," an almost mystical metropolis literally rising from the sea. Neither of her official names truly fits; those of us who live here call Seattle "The Rainy City."

Even so, I love Seattle, unabashedly, unashamedly—so much so that I am tempted to stoop to kiss the tarmac at Seattle-Tacoma International Airport each time I come back from the trips that have become a constant part of my life. So far, I have resisted the impulse.

Seattle—old and new—is astounding from the air. I look down to see the surprisingly narrow stretch of land edged by Lake Washington and the Cascade Mountains to the East, and by Puget Sound and the Olympic Mountains to the West. I can see the Space Needle, toy-sized from this perspective, and beyond it to the southwest the pointed triangle that is Alki Point. The Space Needle is only a quarter of a century old, a soaring reminder of the 1962 World's Fair; Alki is as old as Seattle herself.

Alki—means "Bye and Bye" in Indian language — this was lands' end, the spot where Seattle's founding Denny Party docked in that sodden November in the 1850's.

Today, the young cruise Alki's beach drives, building bon fires, roasting hot dogs. Alki is a fun, party place. More than a hundred years ago, those 10 adults and 12 children

Sunrise on Lake Union

(Opposite) Seattle at night

who were all that made up the Denny Party (originally touted to consist of a thousand people) survived a winter where it rained unrelentingly and hope faltered. "Bye and Bye" indeed. Subsisting on fish and berries and the kindness of Chief Sealth and his people, the territory that was to become Seattle (named for the Chief who saved them) seemed a soaking, grey, dripping wasteland to the Denny Party who longed for their native Illinois. The women cried and longed for Illinois and a dry roof. The men fought stubborn stumps as they cleared a foothold on this promised land.

It still rains. And rains. And rains. If you live in Seattle long enough, rain seems normal, natural, and healthy. We view sunshine with suspicion if it hangs around more than a day or so.

Seattle is cosmopolitan; Seattle is small town. She's ethnic, and continental and funky, and down-home and sophisticated. It all depends on where you are and what makes you comfortable.

*   *   *   *

In many ways, Seattle is the last frontier of major American cities. Located in the furthermost northwest corner of the contiguous United States, there is nothing west but the Pacific Ocean, and, to the north lies the Canadian Border. I always smile when soap-opera writers who seek to send a character to the end of the earth invariably ship him off to Seattle! Never to be heard from again. . . lost in a wilderness of firs and cedars, perhaps even to be devoured by our elusive Sasquatch half/human-half/beast.

Despite east coast writers, we are not in Siberia here. We are alive and well, and even a smidge cosmopolitan.

Seattle is still a young city, a place where anything is possible. Friendly, welcoming, and dynamic, Seattleites are also some of the more civilized, polite people around. In a traffic gridlock (yes, here too), drivers here automatically slow and wave you into line ahead of them. They even slow for pedestrians. Last year, Seattle came in second in the "good manners" category out of all the cities in America.

Seattle is a "Scorpio City—" based on the month she was founded, but she might better be a Pisces. Water dominates the 25 miles of hourglass-shaped land that marks off the city. Beyond the big lake and the Sound, there are waterways lacing the landscape and lakes in the very middle of the city. Even on a downtown street, you can pause and enjoy the clear blue vista of Puget Sound with sea gulls gliding effortlessly over the ferry boats. The tangy smell of sea air salts the breeze.

The Olympic Mountains cut a jagged, crisp line of white and steel blue against the western horizon, so breathtakingly clear that they sometimes seem an illusion close enough to touch. Mount Rainier is really many miles away from downtown Seattle; but, on a clear day, this snow-topped mountain dominates the view. After three decades, I still gasp with delight to see Mount Rainier. She is more lovely with every glimpse.

Yesterday and today co-exist in Seattle. For more than fifty years, the gleaming white art-deco Smith Tower, with its distinctive elevator cages and peaked top, was far and away the tallest building in the city. No more. The Smith Tower has been humbled by the building explosion that has sprinkled skyscrapers all over downtown Seattle. The Columbia Tower, black and square, is 76 stories high, and the tallest building west of the Mississippi was first thought to be a potential hazard to aviation space. It is a gleaming obelisk of ebony and the Smith Tower is but a mushroom at its feet. There are others, built of glass, built of blue and white tile, built as one reviewer said, "of steel and skin." To date 11 buildings in downtown Seattle are more than 40 stories high.

The Conservatory at Volunteer Park

The Japanese Gardens

Some of us approve of the tall buildings; others do not. Many admire the Washington Mutual Tower with its aqua and white design hinting a bit at the past; some hate the steel and glass of the Pacific First Federal Center. Seattleites are vocal in their opinions. However, a compromise exists. As long as the park spaces remain, and as long as new parks are built, the buildings can stay.

I've mentioned rain, but I must admit now that there are many, many days when the sky above is a clear azure blue—just as Perry Como described it as he sang, "The bluest skies you'll ever see are in Seattle!" A growing underground group which has dubbed itself "Lesser Seattle" in a futile effort to hold down population expansion is largely responsible for the widely publicized aspersions on our weather. Surreptitiously, they distribute bumper stickers and t-shirts reading, "Seattle Rain Festival—September to June."

Apparently, their efforts have little effect; an estimated 50,000 people move to Seattle each year. The rumors about rain are all just made up—

Well . . . we do have "Bumbershoot:" a festival held on the Seattle Center Grounds over the Labor Day Weekend, and named to appease the rain gods. It usually works.

Assuming that you are not opposed to rainy days or foggy days, to warm summer days with cool evenings, I think you'll be glad you came to visit—or to live in—Seattle.

Downtown Seattle

Beyond the new buildings, the "old" Seattle remains. Pioneer Square still exists. Indeed, its perimeters have grown. A few steps from the glass towers of the 1980's and '90's, you can walk on aged bricks beneath ornate pergolas. Both Pioneer and Occidental Squares have kept their sense of yesterday. Streets to the south of the Squares have been given over to a happy mishmash of art galleries, bookstores, funky taverns, upscale souvenir and toy stores, and other shops designed to attract the browser on a Sunday afternoon. Real bargains are to be had in shops in the Smith Tower, the Grand Central Building, and the Pioneer Building, along with the little shops on the street.

Old buildings with their gingerbread touches intact abound. Window boxes and planters spill petunias and geraniums from Spring through Fall.

Here, you can feel as if you have stepped into a time tunnel, an illusion helped by the fact that carefully selected Seattle Police Officers, all tall and mustachioed, wear the uniforms of their predecessors at the turn of the century. They work foot patrol to protect the citizenry, but they are also happy to answer questions and pose for pictures.

You can buy a "take out" sandwich and eat it on the benches of Pioneer Square while you watch the tourists and the local habitues (who are far more interesting than most of us) pass by. Or you can eat at one of the many sidewalk cafes. The proud old buildings on the squares have had face lifts and new paint added but their essence remains.

Seattle

The Monorail

The oldest of the old Seattle exists today—underground. Covered over after the holocaust that leveled much of the city in the Great Fire of 1889, Seattle's Underground is a dank and eerie reminder of a time long past, and an absolutely fascinating lure for tourists. The ashes of the lost-forever wood buildings of that first Seattle were scarcely cool before the rebuilding began. Streets were raised from eight to 35 feet, leaving the undamaged structures below just as they had been before, only shut away from the sun.

The late Bill Speidel discovered this underground lost city in 1965, and the curious can take the Underground Tour 360 days a year—beginning at Doc Maynard's Restaurant (an eatery named for one of Seattle's more colorful founders, a man known both for his vision and his vast capacity for the grape.) For an hour and a half, you can see the unrestored area below Seattle's streets. The cost is $4 for adults, less for Seniors and children.

Seattle's Fat Tuesday Celebration, held just before Lent begins, is another event to seek out in the Squares area in old Seattle. Fat Tuesday began in Occidental Square in the late 1970's with a ribald festival that calmer heads and law enforcement quashed, but it came back, only slightly subdued, in 1989. It promises to be an annual celebration and one to brighten up February days—and nights.

The International District is close by with its Hing Hay and Kobe Parks, tiny but exquisite. Uajimaya's is a genuine Japanese supermarket, jam-packed with exotic food items and oriental wonders from toys to dishes. Seattle's Chinatown is the third largest in America, and its restaurants range from "family-style" one room spots with incredibly good—and reasonable—food to large and ornate black, red, and gold rooms where the food is equally good. There are also fine Thai, Korean, Vietnamese, and Philippino restaurants in the district. During Seattle's largest celebration of the year—Sea Fair—Chinatown has a wonderful parade with many of its youngsters supporting a twisting, writhing "dragon"

as it moves down the narrow streets of the International District.

It was in Seattle's downtown area where the term "Skid Road" was first coined. In the early logging days, Yesler Street was a dirty grade where logs were literally "skidded" downhill to the waterfront where they could be moved out by boat. Today, "Skid Road" (or Row) serves as the home of men—and women—who have become lost from the mainstream of life. Yesler is part of their territory and they sit in the park next to the King County Courthouse on sunny days, or visit along the street. It is not, by any stretch of the imagination, a life of great comfort or happiness, but this is the area where Seattle's street people tend to congregate. Yesler is a paved street like any other in Seattle today, and the term "on the skids" now applies to the thousands of homeless people who populate the Skid Roads of any major city.

Along Elliott Bay, walking from Pier 51 to Pier 70 (or riding the old-fashioned street car that runs along that route), you will see myriad wonders—from the nameless "petrified man" in the Olde Curiosity Shop to thousands of items in import stores. You may want to hop a ferry at the terminal next to Ivar's Acres of Clams. You can ride to Bremerton and back or to one of the islands that lie to the west of Seattle—Bainbridge, Vashon.

No look at Seattle's waterfront would be complete without mentioning Ivar Haglund. Ivar began his restaurant empire with his snack bar on Elliott Bay where married men were once forbidden to drink the clam broth without their wives' permission! The snack bar is still there, in front of Ivar's huge restaurant, and hard by the Seattle Fire Department's Harbor station. You can buy fish and chips made from Ivar's original recipe, and toss the leftovers to waiting sea gulls.

Ivar went on to build far more impressive restaurants, and to buy the Smith Tower. He died a few years back, but not without leaving a provision in his will that has continued to pay for the dazzling fireworks display over the Bay on the Fourth of July that was his yearly gift to Seattle.

At Pier 59, the Seattle Aquarium allows you to come nose-to-nose through the glass with such lively creatures as otters, seals, sting rays, octopi, eels, and almost anything else that swims—all in carefully constructed native habitat settings. Waterfront Park allows an unequalled view of Elliott Bay and the off-shore islands from its two-level decks. There, you can fish, sit by the fountain, or just daydream under the trees.

Pier 70 has more shops, restaurants, and dancing to live musical groups.

One of the most popular spots in the waterfront area of downtown Seattle is the wonderfully creaky, original structure that houses the Pike Place Market. Basically sound, the whole market appears to be supported on tall pillars on the Bay side. It clings to the hillside and burrows into it, with an ever-amazing variety of stalls, shops, eating spots. The floors slope, additions are built on willy-nilly, but no new, plumb and square building could ever replace it. Market aficionados fought to save it, and raised money by selling pieces of the market—floor tiles with the name of the contributor.

There may well be nothing in the way of foodstuffs that cannot be purchased in some nook or cranny of the Pike Place Market. Each morning, truck farmers arrive before dawn with produce grown in the rich valley land north and south of Seattle. Some of them have had the same stalls for 50 years. You will be transfixed when you see the rows upon rows of fresh vegetables and fruits, nuts, honey, berries, pumpkins. Free samples and haggling over price are all part of the fun. Bargain hunters know that the prices at the end of the day—and particularly Saturday evening—are the best!

There are barrels of fresh clams, shrimp, Dungeness crabs, and fresh salmon, mussels, every kind of seafood imaginable. There are meat markets, spice shops, tea and coffee shops, real fresh peanut butter spooned into little white cartons (the kind we used to buy goldfish in), baked goods and dairy products. DeLaurenti's International Food Market

Towering new architecture

(Opposite) The new Two Union Square Building

sells bulk pasta, beans and rice, frozen ravioli, manicotti, and fillo leaves for stuffing. Cheese shops have Feta, Jarlsberg, Gouda, Edam, Camembert, Brie, Goat…anything the most exotic taste might seek. Everytime I shop at the market, I stagger out with shopping bags so full that the handles cut into my fingers. But it's worth it.

Independent craftsmen bring their artwork to the market. One table last week had an assortment of exquisite crystals, to be worn for love or luck or good health around your neck on a slender silver chain. Another had cloisonne pins, earrings and bracelets. There are candles, stained glass, Batik, all of good quality and all one of a kind. Sand and oil sculptures move continually into changing moon landscapes as their frames are turned.

For the out-of-towner, or for anyone curious about what is happening thousands of miles away, the newspaper shop at the entrance to the market carries papers and periodicals from all over the world.

Flowers and plants are for sale, and throughout the market, strolling musicians, mimes, and magicians entertain. Regular shoppers and the merchants come to know each other over the years, and pretty girls or grandmothers often are presented with a peach or a bunch of grapes by a gallant green grocer.

(Actually, remembering the Pike Place Market as I write this, I'm tempted to lock up my word processor for the day and go buy some Gerbera Daisies and a little bucket of peanut butter!)

* * * *

If the Pike Place Market clings to its divine antiquity, there is enough new construction in downtown Seattle to more than balance off. One of the more innovative uses for a freeway overpass exists between 6th and 9th Streets (between University and Seneca

Streets.) The Freeway Park is an oasis in the very center of the downtown area. Below, eight lanes of Interstate 5 are continually alive with traffic, but the waterfalls and fountains in the park mute the roars of engines and the squeal of hydraulic brakes. Freeway Park is full of rare—but hardy—evergreen bushes and trees, as well as zinnias, marigolds, petunias, and azaleas and rhododendrons.

You can explore a fascinating walk by beginning up on Seattle's "Pill Hill" where our hospitals and doctors' offices are clustered. Begin at 10th Avenue by walking down gentle elevations of steps, past waterfalls, and then into the park itself. In no time, you will emerge on Fifth Avenue's banking and expensive shop district. The Seattle Park Department provides a free lunch concert for two hours each Tuesday noon during the summer months. At night, colored lights illuminate the Freeway Park's fountains.

A few blocks further north, at 7th and Olive, the new $90 million Washington State Convention Center spans the freeway, a magnificent edifice that offers 371,000 square feet of space. The annual Flower and Garden Show held there draws more than 50,000 people! Movable walls and baffles can accommodate meetings for 50 to 4000 people!

The Westlake Mall is another new building on the Seattle horizon; it opened in October, 1988 and combines downtown shopping with a sense of the public square. A broad expanse of brick-paved open space surrounds the Westlake Center and gives another "stage" for jugglers, bicyclists, singers, and just plain people.

Seattle's Third Avenue has been in disarray for the last few years while an almost-completed bus tunnel 1.3 miles long is being constructed, a rapid transit plan that will ease future inner-city travel.

The Kingdome, home of the Seattle Seahawks and the Seattle Sonics holds forth at the far south end of downtown; Seattle Center is at the north tip. Together, in any logo, the squat Kingdome and the soaring Space Needle of Seattle Center are instantly

The city from Freeway Park

Downtown beauty

24

Peaceful city park

Street vendor

recognizable as *SEATTLE!* Seattle Center is a minute's ride from Westlake Mall's front door on the monorail, 74 acres carefully selected for the 1962 World's Fair so that the buildings constructed would continue to serve needs of Seattle's residents.

The Space Needle, over 500 feet high, has exterior elevators that zoom to the top level in a sometimes stomach-churning 43 seconds. Visitors can stand on the observation deck and see what appears to be the whole world—at least all of Seattle and the Puget Sound region. The Space Needle Restaurant revolves around the top of the Needle, making a complete circle each hour. Diners are treated to a continually changing vista as they eat, yet at a pace so leisurely they need have no fear of sea-sickness.

Something is always happening at Seattle Center—at the Opera House, the Playhouse, where the Seattle Repertory Company presents new plays each season, or in the Pacific Science Center. Seattle has its own symphony orchestra too, but visitors to Seattle Center may find a rock band playing or a lone artist playing a flute under one of the thousands of trees on the grounds. Taste for both visitors and performers is eclectic. As I write this, the Seattle Center has hosted this week both Duran Duran and the Sistine Choir!

Downtown Seattle has a number of hotels, with 6200 rooms available. The hotels range from the understated old world elegance of the Four Seasons Olympic or the Alexis's 54 rooms "in the European Tradition—" to the usual assortment of Sheratons, Marriotts, Hiltons, and Stouffers. I would venture to say that every hotel in downtown Seattle has either been remodeled, built—or torn down—in the last decade.

With rare exception, restaurants are much the same. Ivar Haglund has died, and Victor Rosselini has retired. Grand new "Yuppie" restaurants move in and out of favor. One of the more interesting breakthroughs in eating out in Seattle in the last decade is the advent of the small family-style gourmet restaurants that have appeared in store fronts or in little houses. There are several on Madison Street at the Lake Washington end, and several more along Pine Street. The food is exquisitely prepared and graciously served, even though the spices and accompaniments are so esoteric that mere mortals don't recognize them!

Shilsole Bay Marina

(Opposite) The city across the bay

Seattle's Waterways

Seattle's eastern boundary is Lake Washington, a huge fresh water lake as deep and cold as a mountain lake. Lake Washington extends from Renton at the south end to Kenmore at the north, and separates Seattle from Mercer Island and Bellevue, onetime sleepy little towns—now heavily populated with young families, many of whom work in Seattle. The first bridge to Mercer Island was built in the 1940's and was considered an engineering miracle, floating as it does on pontoons. The second floating bridge, the Evergreen Point bridge, was constructed thirty years later and was so heavily traveled from the start that it was able to suspend its tolls in June, 1979—a full decade before planners had predicted. New construction will soon double the traffic load on the first floating bridge.

From the bridges and the shoreline, drivers and residents are treated to the sight of blossoming spinnakers on sailboats gliding over Lake Washington. On stormy days, the wind whips up the lake so high that it flings itself at the floating bridges, hurtling waves up and over. Nature tamed, but undaunted.

The infinitely dangerous and exhilarating sport of hydroplane racing sends giant "rooster-tails" of backwash high above the lake in late summer when the mighty hydros gather to compete for the Gold Cup. Then, Lake Washington's shoreline is thick with spectators, and pleasure boats, rafts, or whatever-will-floats are tied to log jams along the race course. Seattle's hydro racers are listed prominently in the sport's hall of fame, many of them gone in an instant with one mishap in the sport where boats plane above the water at speeds far over a hundred miles an hour.

For less daring water lovers, there are canoe rides near the University of Washington, smaller hydroplanes racing on Green Lake, and public beaches for swimming all over Seattle and King County. Serious boaters can dock their cruisers and live-aboard sailboats at one of Seattle's proliferation of marinas. Wind-surfing has become a popular water sport on local lakes, and white-water rafting enthusiasts have only a short trip out of town to find suitable rivers to conquer.

To the West of the city, there is, of course, Elliott Bay and then Puget Sound, salt water seas that meander north and south through a continuous series of passages and waterways. There really is no better vista of Seattle than that seen from ferry boats coming into port. I often wonder what the pioneers would think if they could see Seattle today, the city rising majestically out of the mist as the green and white ferries chug steadily east. And even the huge ferries are dwarfed by the thousands of cargo ships that dock at the Port of Seattle every year.

Seattle has reached and far surpassed the potential that the first settlers at Alki envisioned so long ago. "By and Bye" has come and gone and the city continues to grow, along the waterways and so far east that the Cascade Mountains seem to be an eastern boundary.

Lake Union is a landlocked lake just north of downtown. The most optimistic of Seattle's movers and shakers once predicted that the city might even grow until it extended to Lake Union! The city roars by Lake Union for 15 miles more.

Lake Union has long been the site of a particularly "Seattle" brand of lifestyle—the houseboat. Long wooden walkways stretch out to docks from the shorelines of Lake Union—docks lined with floating homes. Little wooden houses they once were, sitting

Seattle through the <u>Changing</u> <u>Form</u> <u>Sculpture</u> on Queen Anne Hill

atop floating logs. Economy housing.

The houseboaters are a community unto themselves, a small town smack dab in the middle of a metropolis. There is a camaraderie and mutual protection society among the water dwellers found nowhere else in the city. A stranger on the dock is questioned — politely but firmly. Dogs aren't usually allowed, but cats and duck families co-exist in the houseboat world.

The early houseboats have virtually disappeared with the "discovery" of houseboat living and the limited number of moorages available. Some of those quaint floating homes are still there, beneath extensive remodeling that heads for the sky, the only space available. Some have been sacrificed for their dock space, and grand homes brought in. It would not be unusual to find a houseboat worth a half million dollars!

Still, a few of the old-timers remain, and neighborliness remains, sometimes taking the form of a unique "community" activity. If logs need to be replaced, a "stringer party" is held — much like an old-fashioned barn raising. The dock is lined with tables sagging with enough food to feed a family reunion, while volunteers dive to replace rotting logs with great blocks of styrofoam. A heavy snowfall is a clear and present danger to houseboaters — and everyone takes to the roofs with shovels before the weight of the snow can cause the floating homes to sink!

Without a stringer party and without the threat of a snow-sinking, there is an annual party along Fairview Avenue East on, of all times, Bastille Day! A pig roasted in a buried pit of coals, casseroles, cakes, pies, and live music draw "invited guests only" for a long day of celebration. An invitation to the houseboaters' Bastille Day Pig Roast is an honor much to be desired!

Houseboat dwellers have no good earth to call their own, so they import soil for planter boxes, hanging baskets, whatever. One of my friends harvests a bumper crop of tomatoes,

Westlake Center

Outside

Inside and . . .

peas, green beans, radishes, lettuce, and even corn—along with every flower imaginable—from her deck garden. Watering is no problem; she needs only to lower a dipper into Lake Union.

A few miles north, there is Green Lake, a bonus for city dwellers. Surrounded by well-kept bungalows of the 20's and 30's, Green Lake lures picnickers, kite flyers, joggers, walkers, skate-boarders, bicyclists, boaters, swimmers, and just plain people who want a beautiful spot to sit and ponder the vicissitudes of life! There is a rule that seems to work: walkers and joggers go one way around the three mile trail, and bikers go the other way. Everyone's considerate, and there are no collisions!

The Seattle Park Department has kept portions of the waterfront dedicated to parks and there is enough park area so that anyone can enjoy the water. Just outside the city, King County Parks offer the same opportunity.

Neighborhoods

Seattle, like most American cities, is a wondrous montage of heritage and custom. I am an inveterate reader of the vital statistics pages of our daily newspapers, and I always marvel to see the ethnic origins of those born and of those who have passed away. You can always be sure there will be Scandinavian names, and Chinese and Japanese names, and German names. In the years since that docking on Alki, Seattle has drawn representatives of almost every culture.

Local comedians pick on Ballard, the northwest corner of Seattle, and torment the Scandinavians there. But then of course, the Norwegians taunt the Swedes and the Swedes tease the Danes. Ballard is one of the solidest communities in Seattle, neat homes, neat lawns, pot-luck suppers and festivals to celebrate Scandinavian customs. Restaurants in Ballard serve Aqua Vit to drink, Lutefisk, and perfectly prepared seafood—as well as steak and prime rib. Commercial fishermen in Ballard follow the calling of their fathers and grandfathers from the old country.

For a look at the most expansive salmon and halibut fleet in America, be sure to visit the Salmon Bay Fishermen's Terminal. It can be found just south of the Ballard Bridge. Commercial fishing vessels of every kind grace the waters here. Trollers, gillnetters, seiners and tenders slice through the chill waters of the bay as fishermen unravel their nets on the weathered docks for repairs. You can buy fresh fish right there on the docks while

Public Market Center at night

you watch gulls wheel lazily overhead, their eyes darting for tidbits. Nearby, sea lions bark, those wily predators waiting to pounce on a meal of salmon. Despite the best efforts of game protectors, the sea lions feast heartily on the mighty fish returning to spawn. Firecrackers, rubber bullets, even trapping and relocation far out into the ocean, have failed to deter the sea lions.

A nautical traffic jam can usually be found on holiday weekends as both pleasure and commercial vessels travel through the Ballard Locks, officially named the Herman Crittendon Locks.

Rocking like so many toy boats in a bathtub, the sea-going craft, large and small, must be hoisted from six to 26 feet (depending on the tide) as they pass through the gigantic locks. $2 million seemed a fortune when the locks were built, but the construction has proved both efficient and aesthetically pleasing, and, in retrospect, a great bargain. Youngsters particularly enjoy the underwater viewing window where they can watch salmon, trout, and steelhead "climb" a fish ladder so close that they can almost reach out and touch them.

Heading due east, you will find the University District, the streets familiar to generations of students who have attended the University of Washington. The campus has grown up and out, but it still retains its sense of wooded paths meandering past buildings that look like castles. In the Spring, the Dogwood and flowering cherry trees, cushions of heather, sweeps of daffodils, and the sweet smell of budding cottonwood trees make the whole campus a magical place.

For a peek at some of the fine old homes in Seattle, take an easy drive east on Madison Street and follow along the lake to the south. The homes are lovely there and range from Colonial to English Norman to Modern. Another good spot for "house-watchers" is along 10th Avenue East just north of the Broadway District. There, you will find the shining white homes with curving driveways, pillars, balconies, leaded glass, and all that early entrepreneurs could build to present to their brides.

The Stimson-Green Mansion, beautifully preserved in every detail, is as grand as ever as it sits on Minor Street at the corner of University. The Mansion can be rented for weddings, receptions, anniversaries or any kind of gathering where elegance and a sense of history can add to the happiness of the occasion.

Speaking of Broadway—this is a neighborhood in a state of revitalization. Broadway, the street, is one of Seattle's most sought-after areas for those seeking a touch of the bizarre, a bit of the funky, and a sense of carnival all year round. An artist has actually embedded bronze dancing feet in the cement along a sidewalk on Broadway. Play hopscotch with them—only do the tango, the waltz, the two-step as the bronzed feet demonstrate.

Broadway is full of restaurants, ranging from Henry's Off Broadway (Valet Parking and expensive cuisine) to the DeLuxe Cafe where they serve, arguably, the best and biggest burgers in Seattle. Broadway has strollers in mink and three piece suits, and it has punk rockers in black satin, sequins, pink hair, and boots. It has art theaters, out-of-town papers, dilapidated taverns, old houses, new apartments, 1950's drive-ins, and New York Italian cuisine. If you want to go somewhere unpredictable—even adventurous, choose Broadway.

Spreading out from Downtown Seattle—where new condos and lofts are rapidly replacing low-rental apartments—Seattle's neighborhoods represent the growth of the city itself. Turn of the century homes on "Pill Hill" and "Capitol Hill," the bungalows of the 20's and 30's in the Fremont, Green Lake, Roosevelt, Ravenna, and the University District, and then the lavish stone and brick homes in Laurelhurst and Windermere, the upscale areas along Lake Washington, all contribute.

After the second world war, the building boom created neighborhoods like Viewridge, Lake Forest Park, Sand Point Country Club, Blue Ridge, and others with winding streets

Seattle, an overview

The city glistens at night

with quaint names. The next building boom would see suburbs springing up in Bellevue, Mercer Island across the lake, north as far as Lynnwood, and beyond Federal Way to the South.

West Seattle is part of the City of Seattle itself, but it sits apart, across the new bridge (the old one was rammed by an errant freighter and mortally wounded.) West Seattle sits on a hill, with water views west, north, and east. Its homes are generally older, its streets wide, and many of its houses sit high up from the street on a plateau, the yards carefully cultivated, the banks to the street planted in groundcover and Juniper bushes. Movie studios often choose West Seattle as a shooting location because it somehow represents the typical medium-sized American town—with magnificent views to boot.

Parks

One of the Emerald City's earliest and most beloved parks—Volunteer Park—sits high atop Capitol Hill. With its sweeping, lavishly landscaped grounds, the park is a wonderfully lush backdrop for any number of functions—both public and private. Free Sunday afternoon concerts in the fresh air offer everything from blue grass to jug bands and rock and roll—to chamber music, flute recitals and John Phillip Sousa. Family and class reunions, barefoot wedding parties, 18th century costume picnics, rallies (political and otherwise), or two lovers holding hands all seem to enjoy the music and the park.

Volunteer Park is also the site of the Seattle Art Museum. The Museum displays art from every possible school and approach with its ever-changing exhibits. Ancient oriental art objects, surrealism, the Wyeth family and their often-startling realism, country art and Picasso. Sooner or later, it will all come around at "SAM."

If the day is cool and both spirit and muscles are in good shape, you may want to attempt the climb to the top of the 75 foot brick tower on the south side of Volunteer Park. At the top of the 106 steps, you can see a 360 degree view of the city spread out below the observation deck.

Long considered to be Seattle's most resplendent display of flowers, shrubs and trees that thrive in the Northwest, the Arboretum (near the University of Washington) reflects each season as the months pass. Rhododendrons, azaleas, magnolias, heathers—from

The old and the new

The best view in town from Rizal Park

The Kingdome

white to dark purple—mountain laurel, dogwood, vine maple brilliant coral in autumn, lilac and lily, willow and wisteria, every growing thing possible—all flourishing near the meandering roads that wind through the Arboretum.

The Japanese Tea Garden, four acres of tranquil ponds, delicate bridges, and vivid flowering shrubs are meticulously designed to transport the visitor's imagination to Japan. The ancient tea ceremony itself is offered to visitors.

To the West again, Gasworks Park nudges Union Bay—an oddly-named park with a peculiar charm all its own. Once a functioning utility complex for old Seattle, the abandoned remnants of the old gasworks have been incorporated into a park for children of the 80's and 90's. Gasworks Park is a must-stop spot for children who will love to explore its intriguing climbing and crawling structures.

Marymoor Park is in the Seattle eastside suburb of Redmond, and the largest park in King County. Athletes can enjoy football and soccer fields, tennis courts, and the state's only bike velodrome! Built as a showplace in 1904, the Clise Mansion and its windmill still stand proudly today in the heart of the park.

Woodland Park, near Green Lake, is home to Seattle's zoo, a complex much admired by zoo afficionados. In the past decade, Seattle's taxpayers and school children's pennies have allowed Woodland Park Zoo to expand and improve so that the exhibits and habitats created adhere faithfully to the animals' origins. The African Savannah, the Swamp, the Marsh, the Asian Primates' and Gorillas' houses, the Nocturnal House, are all amazingly recreated. Seattle's elephants, once scrunched into too-small confines, now move easily through a grand edifice constructed just for them.

Woodland Park is open daily year round, and also features a petting zoo of baby animals for youngsters and a children's theater.

Freeway Park

Green Lake Park

Convention Place

Seattle Art Museum

The Seattle Yacht Club

Aurora Bridge, Lake Union

University of Washington

The student body

Woodland Park Zoological Gardens

"Hi There…"

Hippo's delight

Pier 70 at night

Ivar's

Ivar Feeding The Gulls

The Popcorn Wagon at Seattle Center

Pacific Science Center

The Seattle Mariners©
Photo courtesy of the Seattle Mariners

(Opposite) Seattle Seahawks©
Photo courtesy of the Seattle Seahawks

A few perspectives...

The famous Space Needle

Out-of-Town Trips

If you set out from the center of Seattle, you may head in almost any direction, and find uncountable things to do and places to see all within two to four hours' travel time.

Deep-sea fishermen can drive to Westport where Grays Harbor opens into the Pacific Ocean. "The Salmon Fishing Capital of the World" has some 350 charter fishing boats with skippers ready to help the beginner or the experienced fisherman. Salmon is the catch of choice, but, if you get your limit, your skipper will take you to another site to troll for tuna or bottom fish.

Beyond salt water fishing, there are myriad lakes, rivers, and streams within easy driving distance of Seattle where freshwater anglers can try their luck.

For a bird's eye view of Seattle City Light's colossal hydro-electric project, catch the City Light Skagit tour. The tour includes an excursion up an incline railway, a look inside the Ross Dam powerhouse, a close-up view of the North Cascade mountain range, and a boat ride on Diablo Lake. Despite its name, Diablo Lake is as serene and lovely as the skies of heaven and is such an impenetrably brilliant blue that it dazzles the eye, a "gem" thrown into the mountains' hollows.

For a genuine ocean voyage to another country—there and back, *all in a single day*—board the ferries that cruise north to Victoria, British Columbia. The Princess Marguerite arrives on the picturesque island in four hours. A quicker trip is available by hydrofoil.

A daily 10 a.m. departure time is guaranteed by the ferry services, on vessels large enough to accommodate trucks and campers. Ships also depart later.

In Victoria, the dowager of all grand hotels, The Empress, offers a genuine high English tea with strawberries and cream, petit fours, and buttered bread with cunningly trimmed crusts. A look into another world. The Empress is being refurbished to recall her grandest era. After tea, you must take a stroll through exquisite formal gardens, walk along the sea walls, shop at the little foreign stores, and gaze at the government buildings, their copper roofs green now with the patina of time.

Bed and breakfasts will allow you to stay over if you like, or you can catch an evening ferry back to Seattle.

Within sight of Seattle is Blake Island, a tiny body of land in Puget Sound—famous for its Tillicum Village Indian salmon bakes. Tour boats, rented to groups or to individuals and couples, glide lazily toward Blake, and deposit visitors on a long pier, all of them hungry for the magnificent feast that awaits.

In Tillicum Village, the pits are full of glowing alder coals, and whole salmon, butter-flied, have cooked slowly over the sweet smoke, just the way the Indians did it. First, there are freshly harvested butter clams, and then hot breads, salad, and the mouth-watering salmon—to be followed by wild blackberry pie! The authentic Indian longhouse is full of artifacts to be perused. And then the dancers perform, majestic in the old-time costumes. No longer men, they become the Raven, the Bear, and the Wolf as they dance.

East of Seattle, breathtaking Snoqualmie Falls can be viewed from various vantage points where the spray of the cataract sparkles in the air—or from the more comfortable dining room tables of the new, and plush, Salish Lodge. Overnight accommodations and lavish meals of native fish, fowl, and beef (and gourmet cuisine) are offered.

Mount Rainier is 14,411 and one half feet above sea level (more than a foot and a half

(Opposite) Lighthouse at Discovery Park

<u>Waiting</u> <u>For</u> <u>The</u> <u>Metro</u>

taller than surveys before 1989 indicated!) and is one of the highest mountains in the contiguous 48 states. Only a few hours by car from Seattle, the mountain is much favored by hikers and climbers. There are restaurants, snack bars, and overnight facilities. Mount Rainier's Paradise Inn is not very different than it was when visitors to the mountain marveled at its grandeur six decades ago.

Mount Rainier draws climbers from all over the world, a challenge to those who would joust with nature. Climbing its icy walls and treacherous snow fields is not for the untrained or unprepared climber. Fortunately, wooded trails lace the mountainside at lower elevations, drawing hikers who simply want to commune with nature—and not to conquer it!

(Other quaint hostelries for those who have tired of shiny new hotels are the Lake Crescent Lodge along Route 101 west of Port Angeles, and the Lake Quinault Lodge—also on 101—but you will have to check a map first to see that 101 is fully open from the most northwesterly part of the Olympic Peninsula south, and then east through Indian reservations. All these lodges have huge fireplaces, carved chairs, and furniture built to suit a larger scale of living.)

Bremerton is an exhilerating 55-minute ferry ride from Seattle, a Navy town full of modern and historic tales of the sea. Noted for its huge Navy Yard, Bremerton is the permanent home for the USS Missouri on whose decks the Japanese surrendered to General Douglas MacArthur in 1945. The great Missouri is open to the public.

The ferry trip itself is a large part of the charm of a visit to Bremerton. Some of the region's most beautiful scenery can be enjoyed from the ferry's windows—or from the deck for those who can take the bracing wind. Hilly rich green landscapes, sprinkled with cozy homes can be seen as the ferry glides through Elliot Bay, Rich Passage, and Sinclair Inlet. Looking toward Seattle from the Bremerton (or the Bainbridge Island) ferries, the Emerald City rises above the water line—a magical city of spires, obelisks, soaring buildings, and hills, all of it carved out from the forests of a hundred years ago.

Who among the pioneers could ever have foreseen *this* Seattle?

Skiers flock to Snoqualmie, Stevens, White Pass, and Crystal Mountain from November through March—in a good snow year—all easy one day turnaround trips.

Between Spring and Fall, the mountain passes take on gradually changing qualities. The snow melts from all the highest peaks, and the vegetation comes alive—even the towering evergreens on all sides become bright new green at their tips. As Summer closes down, the pastels of May and the greens of summer turn fiery red, gold and orange. October in the mountains.

There are hundreds of lakes hidden high up in those mountains, some of them visible only from a plane. Others beckon to climbers who consider it well worth the effort to reach them. Private oases await where hikers can shuck their clothes, swim in a cool, azure lake, and then sit in one of "nature's hot-tubs—" underground hot springs bubbling from rocky basins.

Seattle was only one of many cities predicted to become major ports in the 1800's. Tacoma was actually the city considered to have the greatest future. But fortune and commerce are fickle. Many of the other port cities have been preserved, suspended in time. For an intriguing day trip, visit on of the lovingly maintained towns.

Trumpeted as *the* future metropolis of Puget Sound, Port Townsend was a booming little city in the 1880's. On the very northeast tip of the Olympic Peninsula, this port city boasted six banks, three street railroads, and a natural harbor bested only by New York City's! But all its fine dreams were crushed in the crash of 1890, and today Port

Farmers Market

Smith Tower, Pioneer Square

Townsend is a drowsy, nostalgic little town, haven to poets and artists, a town whose grand dreams never quite came true — a Victorian spinster left with memories and dried roses.

Many of the mansions exist today, relics of the magnificence of another age. Proud old homes they are, freshly painted, replete with turrets, elaborate lacy trim, and widows' walks, their green handkerchief lawns edged with red and white petunias. Some of them are rumored to be haunted — and well they may be — by the women who waited for men who never came home from the sea. Visitors to open houses, all sensible people, tell of feeling a blast of cool air, of seeing ribbons untied by unseen hands.

Who knows?

A short ferry ride west from the northern boundary's end of Seattle, Port Gamble recalls its days as a booming lumber town. The company buildings, company store, and the tidy little boxlike workers' houses still stand. Situated on Hood Canal just where it flowed into the Strait of Juan de Fuca, the little town seemed the ideal spot for lumber barons to make their fortunes. It all should have lasted, but somehow it didn't.

Many of the early industries of old Seattle and the cities around her have faded away with the years, but others have eagerly taken their place.

Seattle's founding fathers, enchanted by the possibilities of the harbors and waterways, predicted greatness for their city, but they never heard — or even imagined — such a thing as a machine that flew in the air. And yet it was the airplane that would become the solid bedrock foundation of Seattle's economy. The Boeing Company has grown from a tiny business to become one of the top — if not *the* top plane manufacturer in the world. They work under billion dollar contracts to supply their mighty jets to airlines everywhere.

Boeing's Everett complex, 30 miles north of Seattle, is the site of one of the world's biggest buildings. Inside of the mammoth hangar, a viewing platform allows guests to observe the construction of one of Boeing's huge airplanes.

My favorite trip—although it might not be strictly classified as a "day trip—" begins with a drive across Snoqualmie Pass into eastern Washington to the apple growing region of Chelan County—a three hour trip, although you may want to stay over because the boat uplake leaves early.

In Chelan, board the *Lady of the Lake* at 8:30 a.m. for the four hour trip "up-lake" to Stehekin. Stehekin is a tiny community that edges the northern end of Lake Chelan. There are no telephones, no movies, no roads there. No worries there.

The lodge has an excellent restaurant, the facilities are comfortable—but not lavish— and the world slows down to a pleasant hum while you visit Stehekin. Once it was the spot where the very rich of the last century traveled to visit the famous Field Hotel, all its velvet, silk, gold, and crystal chandeliers brought in by barge. Now, that hotel is under the lake, flooded when Lake Chelan was raised in 1927. For a lover of things past, secrets untold—and I *am* that—there is no better spot for a short vacation than Stehekin.

A closer trip for visitors to Seattle is a tour through the world famous Chateau Ste. Michelle Winery near Woodinville (a few miles north of Kirkland at the end of Lake Washington). Fashioned after a French country estate, the winery is applauded by wine connoisseurs. A free tour reveals each step of wine making—from the arrival of the grapes, fresh from the vineyards of Eastern Washington—to the end product. There is also the final, and *best*, stage: tasting!

* * * *

So this, then, is Seattle—along with something about her close neighbors. Seattle is

Puget Sound sunset

mountains and water and boats and planes and art and music and classics and nostalgia and a kind of fey sense of humor. Seattle is polite, welcoming, cosmopolitan and countrified. Seattle is for those who love cool clean air, flowers, rain, wind in high trees, crashing waves, and quite tea gardens. And Seattle is especially for those who yearn to know the past, to feel a little bit of what the pioneers felt when they set out so bravely, perhaps so foolishly and naively, more than a hundred years ago. They found Seattle. When they passed on, the rest of us came along to carry out their dreams.

But they still walk here: Chief Sealth, and the Dennys, the Lowells, Doc Maynard, the Terrys, the Borens, and all those who came to settle this fledgling city on the edge of the sea, on the edge of the forest.

About the Author

Full-time author, lecturer and criminologist, Seattle based ANN RULE is a very active and talented lady. With over 1400 articles in national magazines and the leading newspapers across the country, one would wonder when she found the time to raise a family of five, lecture and teach seminars and still publish seven books!

And just look at the books; *The Stranger Beside Me* (about Ted Bundy—now in its 21st printing, approaching 2 million copies sold, and currently on best-selling lists). Others include *Possession, Lust Killer, The Want-Ad Killer,* and *The I-5 Killer.* Her latest, *Small Sacrifices,* has spent several weeks as Number 1, non-fiction paperback on the New York Times best-seller list and ended up being on the list nine months. It was also the third book on Publishers' Weekly "longest on their best-seller list" for 1988—and is being made into a two part mini series for ABC Television—starring Farrah Fawcett as Diane Downs.

After all this, why *Beautiful America's SEATTLE?* "Because I love Seattle, it is my home and my favorite city and besides—I like having something truly beautiful for my fans that isn't all murder and killing and *Beautiful America's SEATTLE* is it!"

The ever-present Mt. Rainier

Rear Cover, The Japanese Gardens